19.95

JY - - '13

GREAT BATTLES OF THE CIVIL WAR

by Katie Marsico

ROURKE PUBLISHING
Vero Beach, Florida 32964

www.rourkepublishing.com

Photo credits: North Wind Picture Archives, cover, 11, 44 (bottom); Mark Taylor/iStock Photo, cover, 5, 13, 21, 29, 37; The Print Collector/Photolibrary, 4, 23 (right), 25, 26, 30 (right), 43 (top), 43 (bottom); North Wind Picture Archives/Photolibrary, 6, 8, 9, 16, 32, 33, 34, 40, 42 (bottom), 44 (top), 45; Library of Congress, 10, 12, 14, 15 (left), 15 (right), 17, 18, 20, 23 (left), 24, 27, 30 (left), 36, 39 (left), 39 (right), 41, 42 (top), 42 (second from top), 42 (second from bottom), 43 (second from top); Bettmann/Corbis, 28; Red Line Editorial, 35, 47

Editor: Melissa Johnson
Cover and page design: Becky Daum
Content Consultant: Brett Barker, Assistant Professor of History, University of Wisconsin–Marathon County

Library of Congress Cataloging-in-Publication Data
Marsico, Katie, 1980-
   Great battles of the Civil War / Katie Marsico.
      p. cm. — (Events in American history)
   Includes bibliographical references and index.
   ISBN 978-1-60694-446-2 (alk. paper)
   1. United States—History—Civil War, 1861-1865—Campaigns—Juvenile literature. I. Title.
   E470.M37 2010
   973.7'3—dc22

                                             2009018090

Printed in the USA

ROURKE PUBLISHING

www.rourkepublishing.com - rourke@rourkepublishing.com
Post Office Box 643328 Vero Beach, Florida 32964

Table of Contents

Chapter One

The First Shots Fired

In 1861 the United States was in crisis. Much of the North wanted to stop slavery from spreading. Much of the South felt the North was taking away their right to make decisions. Tensions were rising among the states. Abraham Lincoln had been elected president in the fall of 1860. The South saw Lincoln as a threat to slavery. Beginning in December 1860, southern states began to **secede** from the **Union**. They formed a new country known as the **Confederacy**. The Civil War was about to begin.

Fort Sumter sits in the harbor of Charleston, off the coast of South Carolina. In early 1861 the fort was not even finished when the first shots of the Civil War rang out. The Union and the Confederacy both wanted to control the fortress. As southern states left the Union, they took control of the forts within their borders. Only four

Abraham Lincoln led the Union during the Civil War.

forts remained under Union control in the spring of 1861. Fort Sumter was one of them. Although South Carolina had seceded in December 1860, Fort Sumter still belonged to the Union.

James Buchanan was still president in January 1861. He ordered that troops and supplies be sent to Major Robert Anderson, the U.S. army commander who controlled the fort. A ship tried to reach Sumter with food, weapons, and soldiers on January 9. Confederate forces along the Charleston shoreline opened fire. No one was injured or killed, but the supply ship turned around. Anderson was

This map shows the states that seceded during the Civil War.

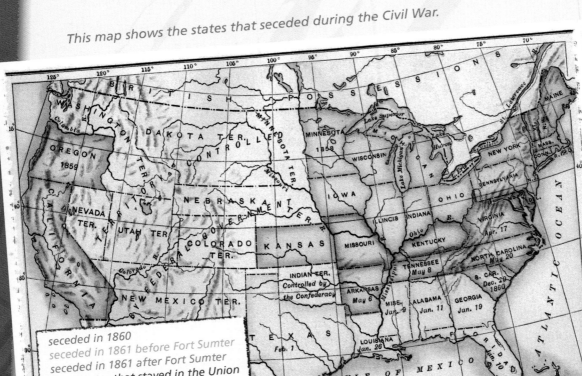

seceded in 1860
seceded in 1861 before Fort Sumter
seceded in 1861 after Fort Sumter
slave states that stayed in the Union
free states that stayed in the Union

left empty-handed. Everyone wondered what would happen next.

Abraham Lincoln took office on March 4, 1861. He became president in the middle of the crisis. Lincoln realized that Anderson would run out of supplies by the following month. Lincoln doubted that Confederate officers would allow more supplies in. They had already ordered the Union to abandon the fort. Nonetheless, Lincoln sent five warships and three tugboats into Charleston's harbor in April 1861. Lincoln notified South Carolina's governor of his plans. Unless the Union was attacked, the president would send only supplies to Fort Sumter, not troops.

> "I sprang out of bed. . . . And on my knees . . . I prayed as I never prayed before. I knew my husband was rowing around in a boat somewhere in that dark bay, and who could tell what each [shot] accomplished of death and destruction?"
>
> —Mary Chestnut, wife of the Confederate soldier who delivered Beauregard's message to Anderson, on hearing the cannon fire at Fort Sumter

Brigadier General P. G. T. Beauregard led the Confederate troops in Charleston. On April 11, 1861 he again ordered Anderson to **surrender** the fort. Anderson refused. However, Anderson admitted that he would have to abandon the fort within days because he was out of supplies. Beauregard was not happy with this answer. His men opened cannon fire beginning at 4:30 the following morning.

BRAVING THE BLAZE

The Union forces at Sumter also faced several fires in the fort. Shots from Confederate cannons set the fort's wooden barracks ablaze. Despite the panic and danger the soldiers faced, they often risked their lives to make sure that the American flag still flew over the fort. Even after surrendering, Union troops proudly raised the flag one final time during a cannon salute. Two Union soldiers were killed when a cannon being used for the salute exploded. Union troops took the banner with them as they left Charleston's harbor.

At first, Anderson attempted to fight back. His efforts were useless. He had too few cannons and guns. The ships Lincoln had sent arrived at the entrance to the harbor, but none could dock during the attack. Fewer than 100 Union troops faced Beauregard and his 500 men. The Union surrendered 34 hours after Beauregard began the **siege**.

No one was killed during the attack. However, two Union soldiers died accidentally from a cannon

Fort Sumter was ruined by the 1861 attack.

The Confederates attacked Fort Sumter on April 12, 1861.

salute after the fort surrendered. The events at Fort
Sumter stirred both the Confederacy and the Union to
gather men and supplies. Both sides prepared to fight for
their beliefs. Lincoln soon asked the states for 75,000
soldiers to crush the rebellion. Four more southern states
seceded. The Civil War had truly begun.

CIVIL WAR QUICK FACTS

- More than 3 million Americans fought in the Civil War.
- More than 620,000 soldiers died, which was 2 percent of the nation's total population.
- At least 185,000 African Americans fought for the Union, making up 10 percent of the army by the end of the war.
- General Robert E. Lee was asked to lead the Union army before he joined the Confederacy when his home state of Virginia seceded.
- West Virginia was part of the state of Virginia before the Civil War. When Virginia seceded from the Union, the counties of West Virginia seceded from Virginia.

The shots fired at Fort Sumter were only the beginning of a long and bloody conflict. Issues such as slavery separated the North from the South while they fought each other for four long years. Thousands of battles large and small were filled with acts of bravery. The lives of hundreds of thousands of soldiers

Major Robert Anderson was the Union commander of Fort Sumter.

Major Anderson saved the Union flag when he surrendered the fort.

were lost. The Civil War changed the course of U.S. history. These epic battles are still remembered more than a century later.

"Gentlemen . . . if you do not batter the fort to pieces about us, we shall be starved out in a few days."

—Anderson's reply to Beauregard, on the surrender of Fort Sumter

Chapter Two

Fighting at Bull Run

Union troops had suffered a loss at Fort Sumter. Still Lincoln and several of his commanders hoped that the war would not last long. They hoped the revolt would be ended with a few battles. The leaders were confident that they could **blockade** the South, using the Union navy to close the South's ports so no ships could enter or leave. They also wanted to capture the Confederate capital of Richmond, Virginia. They called it the Anaconda Plan because they hoped it would strangle the South, like the snake called the anaconda does to its prey.

Meanwhile the Confederates were equally optimistic that they would quickly win. The First Battle of Bull Run made it clear that the war would last a long time. In the summer of 1861, General Irvin McDowell led between 28,000 and 30,000 Union troops from Washington D.C.

Most of the troops at the First Battle of Bull Run had little training.

THE VALUE OF VICTORY

It was important for the Confederacy and the Union to win seaports and railway stations. Ships and trains could transport supplies, weapons, and soldiers across the country. The winning army at the First Battle of Bull Run would gain an important advantage. The fighting took place just a few miles north of Manassas's railroad crossing. It would allow whoever controlled the area to send supply trains throughout Virginia and beyond.

toward Richmond. The men had not trained for battle very long. But Lincoln wanted the Union army to strike a quick blow to the South. He hoped this would end the fighting.

The Union troops marched south from Washington D.C. The officers had little experience keeping the men in line. The troops had little training. Soldiers left their spots in line to pick berries and to rest. It took them more than two days to march 22 miles (35 kilometers).

The Union and the Confederacy both fought to control supply routes and railways.

General Irvin McDowell led the Union forces at the First Battle of Bull Run.

Brigadier General P. G. T. Beauregard led the Confederate forces at Fort Sumter and at Bull Run.

BATTLE SPECTATORS

A number of people came to watch the First Battle of Bull Run, including reporters and congressmen and their families from Washington D.C. Many of them thought the battle would end the war that day. They were unprepared for the grim reality of war and were shocked when the Union lost the battle. Their carriages blocked the roads leading from the battlefield and got in the way of the Union army leaving the battle.

Later in the war, armies would often march that distance in one day.

On July 21, 1861 McDowell came face-to-face with approximately 22,000 Confederate forces. They met at Bull Run, a stream flowing about 30 miles (48 kilometers) west of Washington D.C.

The Brigadier General P. G. T. Beauregard, who had won at Fort Sumter, helped lead the Confederates. They advanced from their base at Manassas Junction in

The Confederate troops rally at Bull Run.

Confederate General Jackson held the Union soldiers back at the First Battle of Bull Run in 1861.

Virginia. For this reason, the First Battle of Bull Run is also called the Battle of Manassas.

BACK TO BULL RUN

Bull Run saw more fighting about a year later. From August 28 to August 30, 1862, the Second Battle of Bull Run raged in Virginia. Once again, the bloodshed ended in a Confederate victory. Even more human life was lost in 1862. The combined number of dead, wounded, captured, and missing for each side was listed at 22,000 to 25,000 men. This was close to five times the total from 1861.

At first it seemed that McDowell had the upper hand. The five-hour fight began shortly after the sun rose. He drove the Confederates across the stream. They went southward to Henry House Hill, which was not far from Bull Run. However, Confederate General Thomas J. Jackson was waiting on the hill. He held the Union soldiers back. His troops fought so hard that another

Union troops retreat after the First Battle of Bull Run.

general said, "There is Jackson standing like a stone wall." Ever after, he was called *Stonewall* Jackson. A Union army victory seemed less likely when 9,000 Confederate soldiers joined Jackson later in the day.

Faced with so many fresh enemy troops, the Union fighters began to hesitate. The untrained troops on both sides tired quickly. McDowell's men **retreated** back to Washington D.C. in a disorganized mob. The Confederates were too tired to chase them far. The South had won the First Battle of Bull Run.

Between 2,800 and 3,000 Union forces were listed as dead, wounded, captured, or missing. The Confederate army suffered only about 1,750 to 2,000 **casualties**. Beauregard and Jackson had shattered any Union dreams of a fast and easy end to the revolt. The Southerners had shown that they were a force to be dealt with. They were fighting an actual civil war rather than a minor rebellion.

> "I started off for the scene of action to see how the fight was progressing. . . . As I emerged from the woods I saw a bomb shell strike a man in the breast and literally tear him to pieces. I passed the farmhouse which had been [used] for a hospital, and the groans of the wounded and dying were horrible."
>
> —Union Corporal Samuel J. English, describing the fighting at Bull Run

Chapter Three

Deadliest Day

The Confederate army was very strong in the fall of 1862. Confederate General Robert E. Lee decided to push north and launch an attack in Maryland. Until that point, much of the fighting had occurred in the South. Lee believed that a victory in the North would help the Confederacy win control over train and ship routes. The Confederacy wanted Great Britain and France to send help. A Confederate win in Maryland would show that the South could win the war and deserved their help.

Lee ordered his troops to cross the Potomac River in September 1862. He sent some of his soldiers to Harpers Ferry, Virginia and Hagerstown, Maryland. Lee headed to Antietam Creek near Sharpsburg, Maryland.

Union General George B. McClellan pursued Lee to Sharpsburg's cornfields. A Union scout discovered a lost copy of the Confederacy's battle plans. The Union

General Robert E. Lee, shown here in 1865, led the Confederate army.

army caught up with southern troops near the town in mid-September 1862. Union forces attacked Lee's men in local farm fields and woods starting at dawn on September 17, 1862.

Although Confederate reinforcements arrived late in the day and stopped the Union advance, they could not change the outcome of the battle. Roughly 50,000 Confederates had faced nearly 87,000 Union troops. The battle ended with terrible casualties. More than 12,000 Union soldiers and more than 10,000 Confederates were listed as dead, injured, captured, or missing. More American lives were lost in battle on September 17, 1862 than on any other single date in U.S. history.

The Battle of Antietam changed the war. It forced Lee to retreat to Virginia by September 18, 1862. He had to put his plans for a northern invasion on hold. The loss meant that Great Britain and France would not send aid to the South.

George McClellan
led the Union army
at Antietam.

Drummer boys used their drums
to signal orders during battle.
Some drummer boys were as
young as 11.

SHILOH

The Battle of Shiloh was fought on April 6 and April 7, 1862 in Tennessee. The Confederates were led by General Albert Sidney Johnston. They launched a surprise attack on the Union army. Although the Union won, more Americans fell during the two-day battle than during all previous U.S. wars combined.

The Union win allowed Lincoln to announce an **Emancipation Proclamation** on September 22, 1862. This order would free the millions of slaves living in Confederate states. It took effect on January 1, 1863.

Lincoln had waited for a big victory such as Antietam to make the proclamation.

Union troops charge the Confederate position at Antietam.

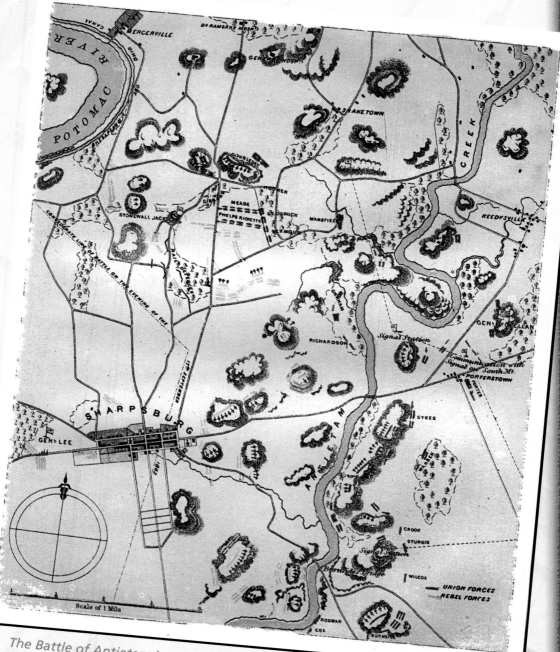

The Battle of Antietam in 1862 was a big Union victory. This map shows the position of the armies at Antietam.

Lincoln's advisors did not want him to give the proclamation while he was losing the war. They thought it would make the president look weak. The win at Antietam helped people believe that the Union could win the war. However, the war was far from over. Soon after, Confederates invaded northern soil in the town of Gettysburg, Pennsylvania.

Freed slaves march north into Union territory after the Emancipation Proclamation takes effect in 1863.

Lincoln meets with General McClellan on the battlefield at Antietam.

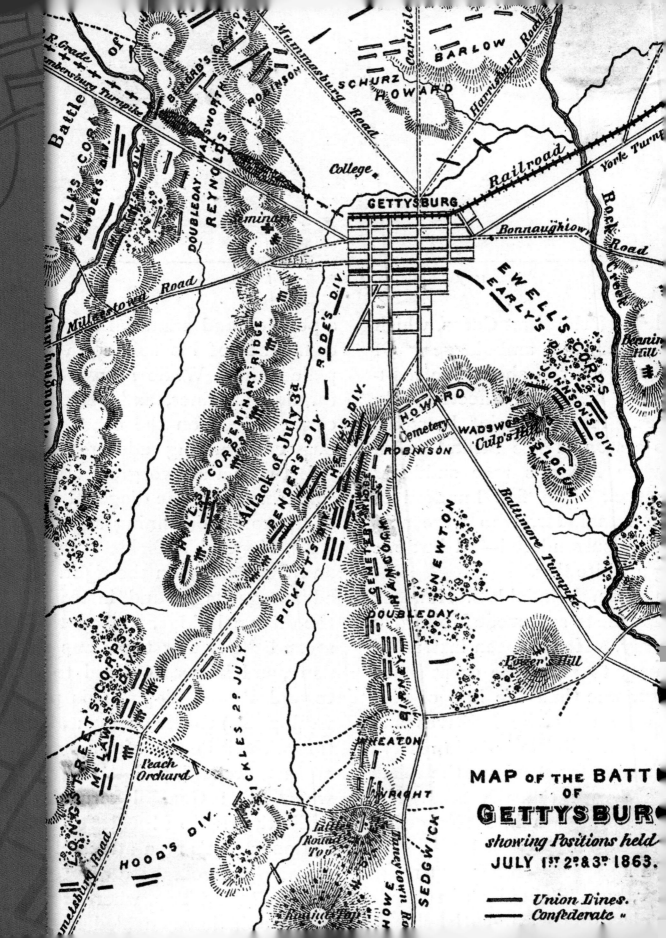

MAP OF THE BATTLE OF GETTYSBURG

showing Positions held
JULY 1st 2d & 3d 1863.

——— Union Lines.
---- Confederate "

Chapter Four

The Turning Point

Confederate General Robert E. Lee failed to invade the North in the fall of 1862. Yet Lee wanted to try again. By the summer of 1863 the war had lasted more than two years. Lee hoped that a big attack in the North would force Lincoln to make peace.

In late June 1863, Lee led approximately 75,000 southern troops northward into Pennsylvania. They moved toward the town of Gettysburg. Meanwhile around 90,000 Union forces gathered under General George G. Meade to meet Lee's men. The Battle of Gettysburg erupted on July 1, 1863 when Confederate soldiers attacked Union **cavalry** outside of town.

During the first day of fighting the southern army seemed to be winning. However, the Confederates only faced a small number of the Union troops in Pennsylvania. They fought for several hours.

The Battle of Gettysburg in 1863 stopped the Confederacy's advance north.

General Meade led the Union forces at Gettysburg.

Soldiers charge through farm fields during the Battle of Gettysburg.

Confederate troops forced the northern soldiers to retreat and took thousands as prisoners of war. As night fell, Meade announced that they would not continue to retreat. Meade realized that the Battle of Gettysburg could be a turning point in the war. If the Confederates won they could continue their invasion.

The battle continued on July 2, 1863. On the second day, southern victory seemed less certain. Meade and Lee faced one another on two ridges that were about one mile (1.6 kilometers) apart. The Confederates began another assault. But they were unable to overtake the Union army.

Lee also understood how important Gettysburg was. On the third day of the battle, July 3, Confederate General George E. Pickett led 15,000 foot soldiers toward the Union line. They faced heavy cannon and **musket** fire. The move was courageous but costly. During Pickett's Charge, as the attack was later called, approximately 10,000 Confederate troops fell.

Lee began to retreat southward on July 5, 1863. Meade and his Union forces had won. Each side had suffered

"I fairly shrank back aghast at the awful sight presented. The approaches [to the farmhouse] were crowded with wounded, dying and dead. The air was filled with moanings and groanings. As we passed on toward the house, we were compelled to pick our steps in order that we might not tread on the . . . bodies."

—Fifteen-year-old Tillie Pierce of Gettysburg describing the aftermath of the battle

VICKSBURG

The Confederate city of Vicksburg was under siege by the Union army during the spring of 1863. The city fell to the Union on July 4, 1863. Losing this city on the Mississippi River divided the Confederacy in half. The northern leader, Ulysses S. Grant, was soon promoted to command the entire Union army.

tens of thousands of casualties. The North counted around 23,000 men as dead, missing, wounded, or captured. The South had lost between 25,000 and 28,000 soldiers. To this day, the Battle of Gettysburg is the largest and bloodiest conflict ever fought in North America.

The Confederate army retreats after Gettysburg.

The Confederates lost more than 10,000 soldiers during Pickett's Charge.

THE GETTYSBURG ADDRESS

Several months after the Battle of Gettysburg the people of the town dedicated a new national cemetery. Lincoln spoke at Gettysburg on November 19, 1863. His speech honored all the war dead. He explained the purpose of the war: to protect equality and freedom. Many people agree that the Gettysburg Address is the best presidential speech in history.

The battle marked the beginning of the end for the Confederacy. Lee could no longer plan a major attack on northern ground. He had to defend the southern states that had seceded from the Union.

The next years would be difficult for the Confederate army. Abraham Lincoln was reelected in 1864 and appointed a talented general,

Lincoln gives his Gettysburg Address, often considered the best presidential speech in history.

The Gettysburg Address

Fourscore and seven years ago our fathers brought forth on this continent a new nation, conceived in liberty and dedicated to the proposition that all men are created equal. Now we are engaged in a great civil war, testing whether that nation or any nation so conceived and so dedicated can long endure. We are met on a great battlefield of that war. We have come to dedicate a portion of that field as a final resting-place for those who here gave their lives that that nation might live. It is altogether fitting and proper that we should do this. But in a larger sense, we cannot dedicate, we cannot consecrate, we cannot hallow this ground. The brave men, living and dead who struggled here have consecrated it far above our poor power to add or detract. The world will little note nor long remember what we say here, but it can never forget what they did here. It is for us the living rather to be dedicated here to the unfinished work which they who fought here have thus far so nobly advanced. It is rather for us to be here dedicated to the great task remaining before us—that from these honored dead we take increased devotion to that cause for which they gave the last full measure of devotion—that we here highly resolve that these dead shall not have died in vain, that this nation under God shall have a new birth of freedom, and that government of the people, by the people, for the people shall not perish from the earth.

Abraham Lincoln gave his Gettysburg Address on November 19, 1863.

Ulysses S. Grant, to lead the Union army. The Confederates grew increasingly hungry and hopeless. Still the Civil War was not yet finished.

Chapter Five

Confederate Surrender

B y the spring of 1865 the war was not going well for the Confederacy. Confederate General Robert E. Lee had once hoped to capture Washington D.C. and win a victory on northern soil. He had given up those dreams. He abandoned the Confederate capital of Richmond, Virginia in early April. His army was out of food and other supplies. Lee's only hope lay in reaching supply trains at Appomattox Station.

Union soldiers had burned the Appomattox trains on April 8, 1865 before the Confederate army could unload them. Next, Lee looked west toward Lynchburg, Virginia where there were more trains. He knew that Major General Philip Sheridan's Union cavalry was closing in on his troops at Appomattox Courthouse. Yet he still believed that he could beat the northern fighters and continue westward.

This Union soldier was unusual because soldiers did not usually bring their families into camp.

At dawn on April 9, 1865 Lee ordered his army to move forward against the Union soldiers. This conflict was later called the Battle of Appomattox Courthouse. At first the charge seemed like a success for Lee. The Confederates managed to break through Union lines. However, more **infantry** soon joined Sheridan. The total number of Union forces grew to more than 120,000 men. The southerners were now surrounded by a much larger Union army. Lee's only option was surrender.

The Confederate commander began exchanging notes with Lieutenant General Ulysses S. Grant. Grant was the head of the Union's military forces. The two men agreed to order their troops to stop fighting. There had already been about 500 Confederate causalities. Union casualties were fewer than 200. The generals agreed to meet at a private home in Appomattox Courthouse later that morning.

Their discussion on April 9, 1865 lasted less than three hours.

It concluded when Lee surrendered all Confederate military equipment. Both leaders respected one another, so Grant allowed the southerners to keep their mules and horses and return home. He provided Lee's men with food and supplies before they departed. He even ordered his own soldiers not to cheer at the defeat of the Confederate army.

General Grant accepted the Confederate surrender at Appomattox Courthouse in 1865.

Grant and Lee met at this house in Appomattox to agree to the terms of surrender.

THE LAST BATTLE

Most experts regard the Battle of Palmetto Ranch near Brownsville, Texas as the last official battle of the Civil War. Union and Confederate forces in Texas knew of Lee's surrender in April 1865. Nevertheless, from May 12 to May 13, 1865 they fought one another anyway. No one is certain what caused the clash, especially since the troops knew the war was over. In the end, Confederate troops won this final conflict. More than 100 men from both sides were captured, while only a dozen were killed or wounded.

Over the next few weeks, there were a few minor battles in other parts of the nation. However, most people agreed that the war had ended at Appomattox Courthouse. Lee had controlled the majority of Confederate forces. Other Southern commanders surrendered soon after. But the years ahead would not bring instant peace to the country.

The South was in ruins. Farms and cities had been destroyed. The North

Lee surrenders the Confederate army to Grant.

Former slaves celebrate their freedom at the end of the Civil War.

and South were still bitter as states gradually rejoined the Union. Five days after Appomattox, a Southerner murdered Lincoln. In addition, millions of newly freed slaves had to fight for basic human rights. The Civil War was followed by a period known as Reconstruction. This was a time of great social and political change for the United States. Life would never be the same again in either the North or the South.

"There is nothing left [for] me but to go and see General Grant, and I would rather die a thousand deaths."

—Robert E. Lee on the surrender at Appomattox Courthouse

Biographies

P. G. T. Beauregard (1818–1893)

Beauregard led the South in several Civil War battles, including Fort Sumter and Bull Run. He served the U.S. Army in the Mexican-American War (1846–1848). Later in life, Beauregard was the president of a railroad and the commissioner of public works in New Orleans.

Ulysses S. Grant (1822–1885)

Grant was a commander of the Union army during the Civil War. He negotiated the Confederate surrender at Appomattox Courthouse. He became president of the United States in 1869. Grant served two terms, ending in 1877.

Thomas Stonewall Jackson (1824–1863)

Jackson was an instructor at the Virginia Military Institute before the Civil War. He received the nickname *Stonewall* because he would not retreat at the Battle of Bull Run in 1861. Jackson died when he was accidentally shot by his own men during the Battle of Chancellorsville in May 1863.

Robert E. Lee (1807–1870)

After a successful career in the U.S. military, Lee took command of the Confederate army during the early 1860s. His surrender at Appomattox Courthouse essentially ended the war. He became president of Washington College in Lexington, Virginia, now called Washington and Lee University.

Abraham Lincoln (1809–1865)

Lincoln was the sixteenth president of the United States. He served from 1861 to 1865 during the Civil War. A quiet, honest politician from Illinois, he was openly against slavery. His election prompted several southern states to secede. Lincoln signed the Emancipation Proclamation. He was assassinated shortly after the Civil War ended in 1865.

George C. Meade (1815–1872)

Meade made a name for himself at the Battle of Gettysburg in 1863. He later worked with Grant, planning military strategies for the rest of the war. Meade served in the U.S. Army until his death, seven years after the end of the Civil War.

George B. McClellan (1826–1885)

McClellan stopped Lee at the Battle of Antietam in 1862. He and Lincoln did not always agree. Therefore, he did not play a major role in the war after Antietam. McClellan ran unsuccessfully against Lincoln for the presidency in 1864. He was governor of New Jersey from 1878 to 1881.

Timeline

December 20, 1860
South Carolina is the first state to secede from the Union.

January 9, 1861
A ship attempts to reach Fort Sumter with supplies, but Confederate forces open fire on the vessel.

April 12, 1861
Beauregard orders his men to open fire at 4:30 AM. The first shots of the Civil War ring out near Charleston, South Carolina.

July 21, 1861 ▲
The First Battle of Bull Run occurs near Manassas, Virginia. The Confederacy wins.

September 22, 1862
Lincoln issues the Emancipation Proclamation.

April 11, 1861
Beauregard orders Anderson to surrender Fort Sumter.

Early January 1861
Buchanan orders that troops and supplies be sent to Major Anderson at Fort Sumter.

April 13, 1861 ▼
Anderson is forced to surrender Fort Sumter after a 34-hour Confederate siege of the fort.

January 1, 1863
The Emancipation Proclamation goes into effect.

September 17, 1862
The Battle of Antietam erupts near Sharpsburg, Maryland. The Union wins, but more American lives are lost in battle on this day than any other in U.S. history.

July 1, 1863
The Battle of Gettysburg begins just outside Gettysburg, Pennsylvania. On the first day of fighting, it appears that Confederate troops have the upper hand.

July 3, 1863
Pickett leads his famous and deadly Confederate charge against Union lines.

November 19, 1863
Lincoln delivers his famous Gettysburg Address.

April 9, 1865
The Battle of Appomattox Courthouse is fought at dawn. Lee begins exchanging notes with Grant to discuss a possible surrender.

April 14, 1865
Lincoln is assassinated in Washington D.C.

July 5, 1863
Lee retreats after losing at Gettysburg. The battle is the largest and bloodiest conflict that ever occurred on North American soil.

July 1, 1863
Late at night Meade announces his decision not to retreat.

May 12–13, 1865
The Battle of Palmetto Ranch near Brownsville, Texas is the final conflict of the Civil War.

April 9, 1865
Lee meets Grant in Appomattox Courthouse in the afternoon. They negotiate Lee's surrender. This discussion essentially ends the Civil War.

April 8, 1865
Union forces burn the supply trains at Appomattox Station in Virginia; the northern cavalry blocks Lee's army.

Glossary

blockade (blok-ADE): to block off an area that is important to the enemy

casualties (KAZH-oo-uhl-teez): soldiers listed as dead, wounded, missing, or captured at the end of a battle

cavalry (KAV-uhl-ree): an army unit made up of soldiers on horseback

Confederacy (kuhn-FED-ur-uh-see): the states that seceded from the United States; the South

Emancipation Proclamation (i-MAN-si-pay-shun prok-la-MAY-shun): Lincoln's order that freed slaves in the Confederacy

infantry (IN-fuhn-tree): an army unit made up of foot soldiers

musket (MUHSS-kit): a long gun carried by infantry

retreated (ri-TREET-id): moved away from enemy forces

secede (si-SEED): leave or withdraw from a group

siege (SEEJ): an act of war that occurs when enemy forces surround a fort or city and attack it

surrender (suh-REN-dur): give up

Union (YOON-yuhn): the states that did not secede from the United States; the North

Websites

Civil War at the Smithsonian Institute
http://civilwar.si.edu/

EyeWitness to History.com— The First Battle of Bull Run
www.eyewitnesstohistory.com /bullrun.htm

Kidport Reference Library - Civil War
http://www.kidport.com/RefLib /USAHistory/

The National Park Service— Gettysburg for Kids
www.nps.gov/gett/forkids/ index.htm

Social Studies for Kids— Battles of the American Civil War
www.socialstudiesforkids .com/subjects/civilwarbattles.htm

Reference Map

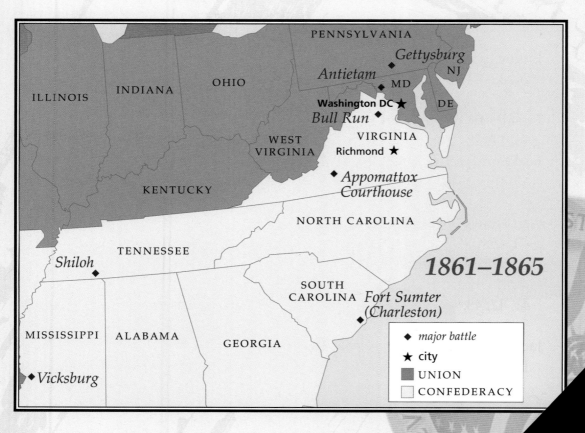

Index

"Follow me, chicks!

Stay close!
PEEP, don't fall behind.

It's a BIG
world out there!"

PEE

A LITTLE BOOK ABOUT

POP!

TAKING A LEAP

Written and Illustrated by MARIA VAN LIESHOUT

Designed by MOLLY LEACH

FEIWEL AND FRIENDS NEW YORK

PEEP marched

TIC-TOC-TIC-TOC

along the edge of the sidewalk
with his mother and sisters.

c-toc-tic-toc-tic-toc-tic-toc-tic-toc

PEEP's sisters hopped off the sidewalk.

PEEP looked over the edge.
"Oh, no!"
he gasped.
"I can't!"

PEEP's legs trembled.

"I'm not sure about this. . . ."

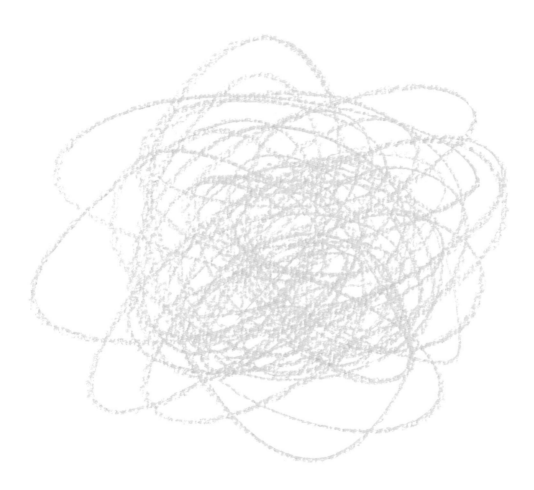

"I don't want to!"

"I don't feel so good.

I'm going home now,
OK?"

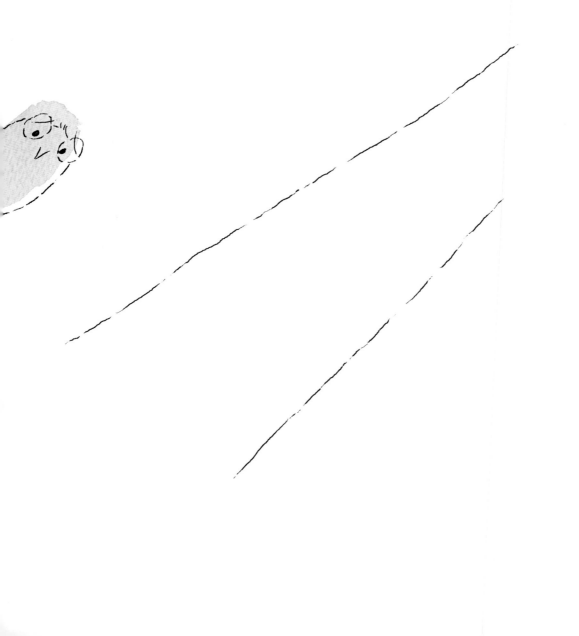

"OK . . . ?"

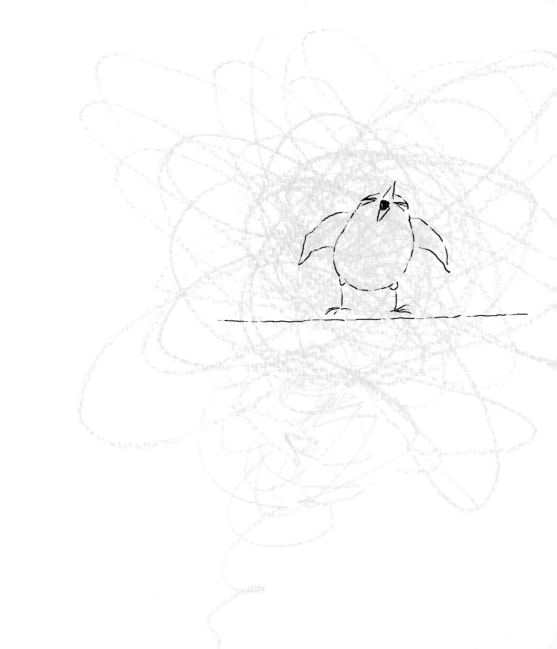

His mother called,
"You can do it, PEEP!"

His sisters cried,

"Jump, PEEP!
JUMP!"

PEEP blinked three times.

He took
a BIG gulp . . .

. . . and SAILED off the sidewalk.

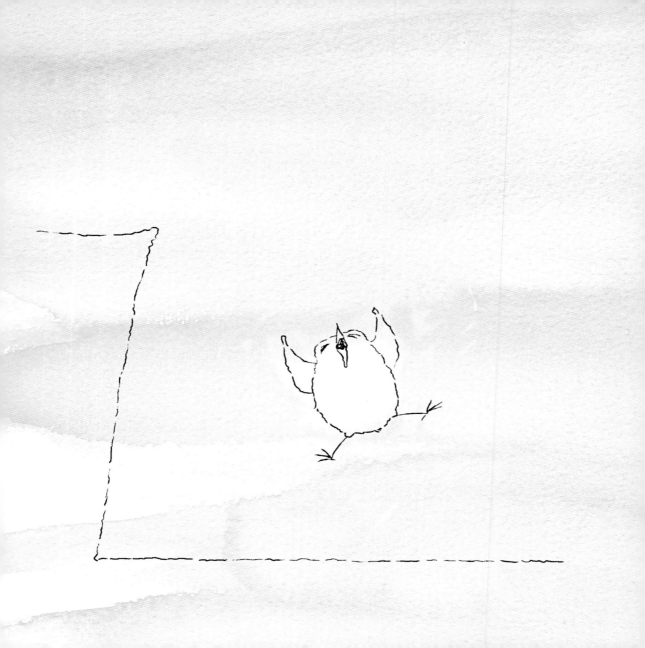

"I DID IT!"

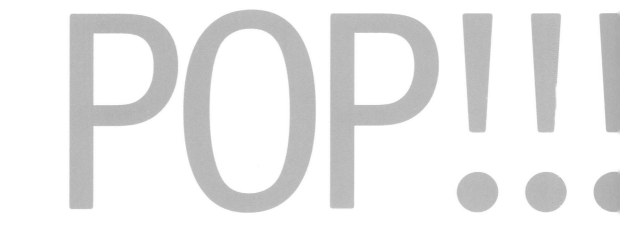

His sisters squealed and kissed him.

PEEP took a deep breath and sighed,
"I did it."

"Uh-oh!"

FOR LIZ SZABLA, MOLLY LEACH, AND STEVEN MALK

A Feiwel and Friends Book
An Imprint of Macmillan

The artwork is created using pencil, ink, and watercolor. First, pencil sketches are traced with ink and scanned into the computer. Then the sketch is placed on a lightbox with watercolor paper so that watercolor may be applied; this watercolor layer is then scanned into the computer as a separate Photoshop layer. The ink line is traced with a writing tablet, and colored pencil is added where necessary.

Library of Congress Cataloging-in-Publication Data Available

ISBN-13: 978-0-312-36915-6
ISBN-10: 0-312-36915-8

Feiwel and Friends logo designed by Filomena Tuosto
Design by Molly Leach

First Edition: March 2009

www.feiwelandfriends.com

10 9 8 7 6 5 4 3 2 1